NAA P-51B-5-NA, Mustang III

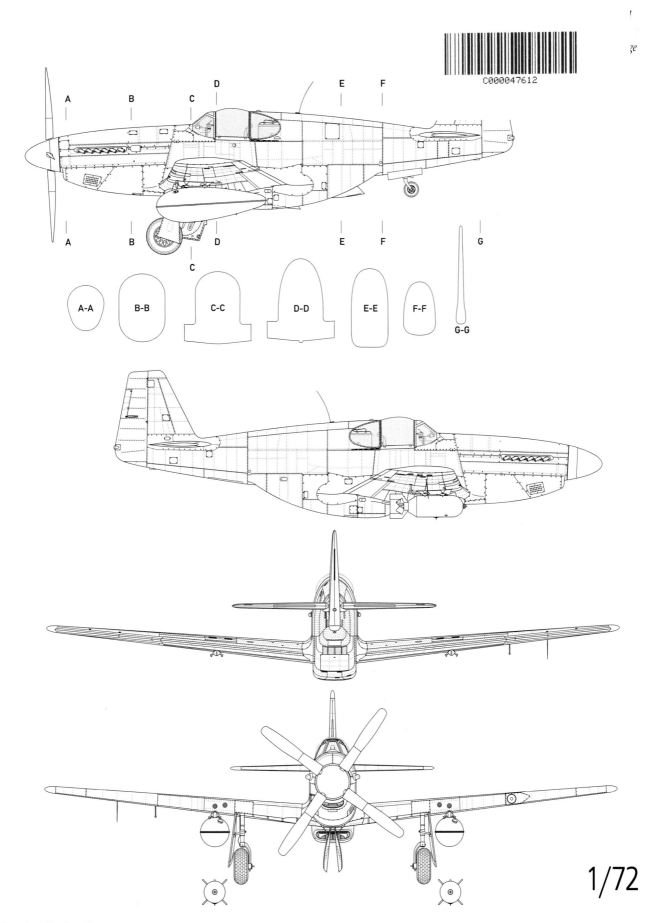

C000047612

A-A B-B C-C D-D E-E F-F G-G

1/72

Drawings: Dariusz Karnas

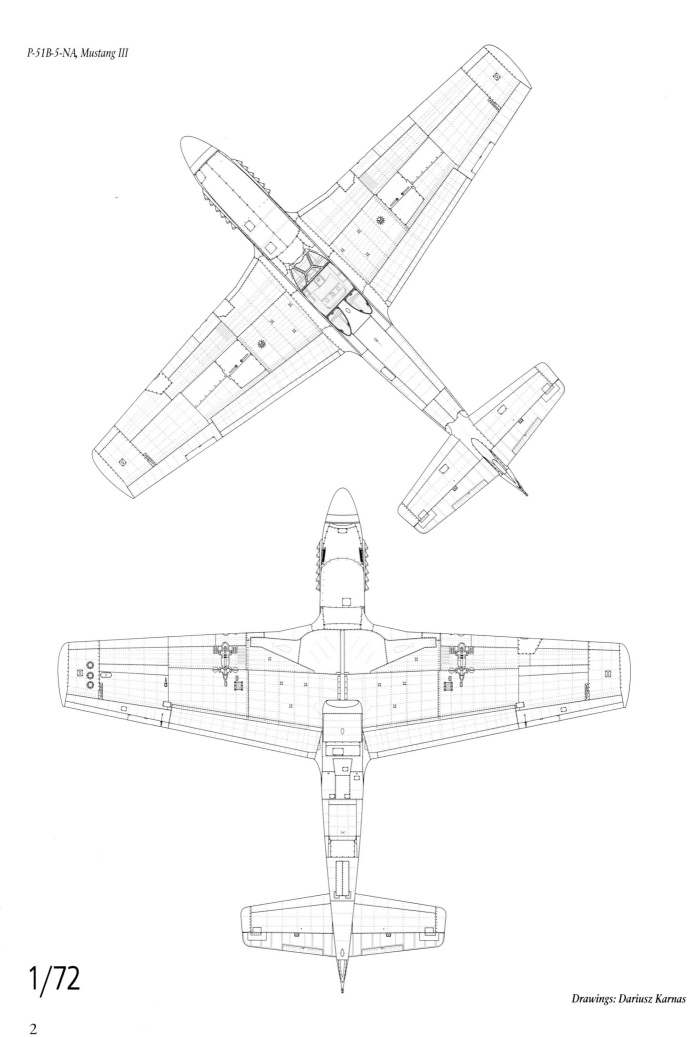

1/72

Drawings: Dariusz Karnas

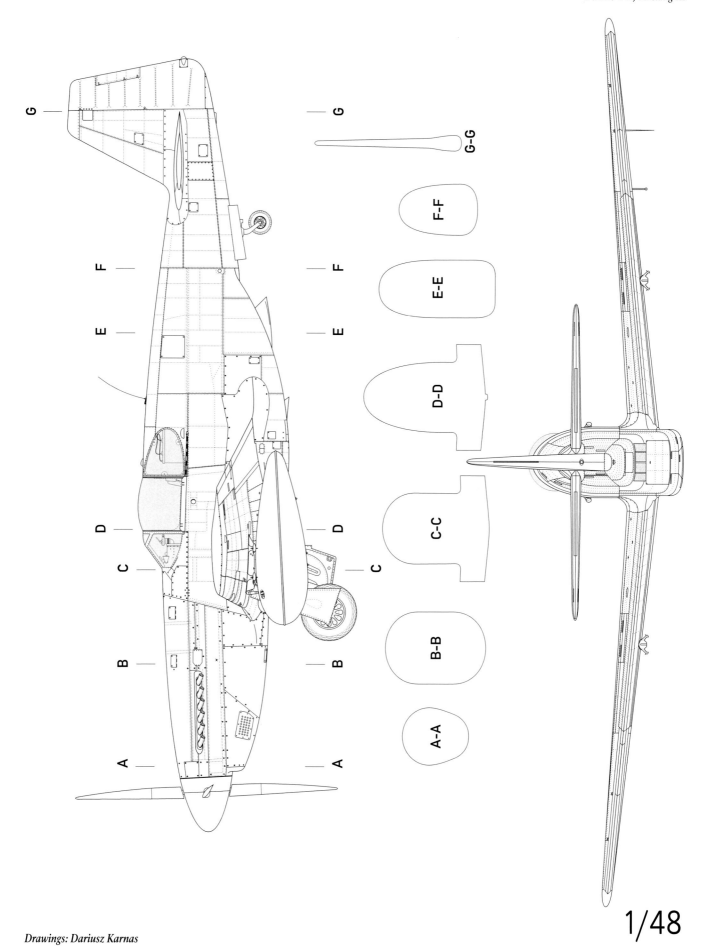

G-G

F-F

E-E

D-D

C-C

B-B

A-A

1/48

Drawings: Dariusz Karnas

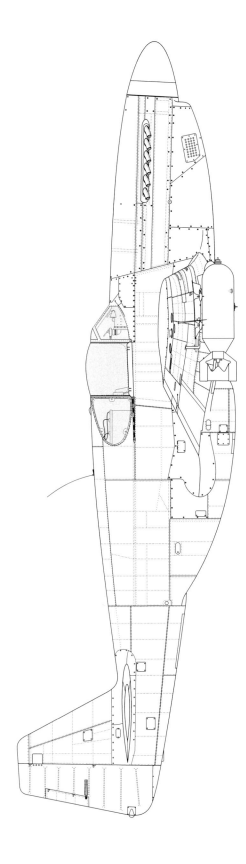

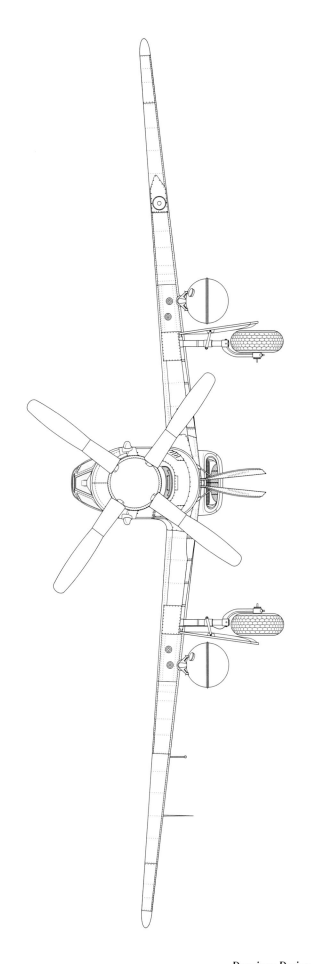

1/48

Drawings: Dariusz Karnas

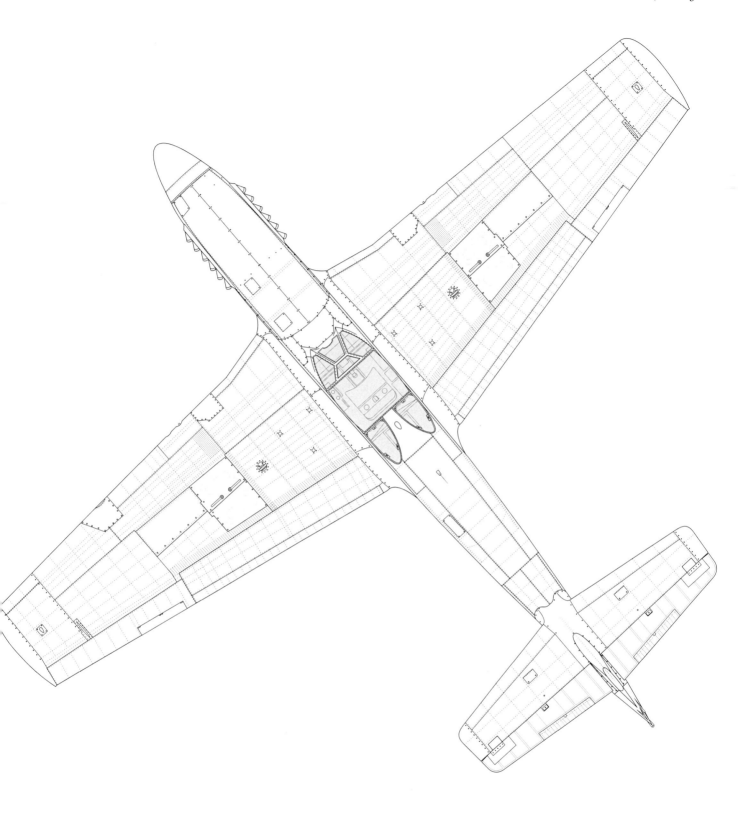

1/48

Drawings: Dariusz Karnas

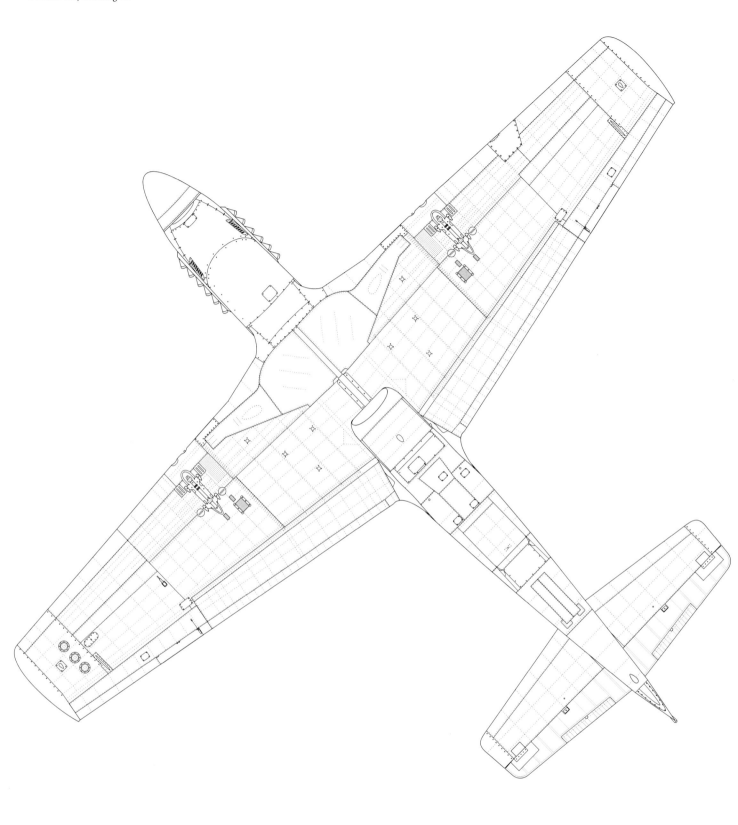

1/48

Drawings: Dariusz Karnas

Mustang III FZ152, SS, (P-51B-5-NA, s/n 43-6533), personal aircraft of Wing Commander Stanisław Skalski when commanded No. 133 Polish Fighter Wing, during refueling, June 1944.

The same aircraft showing Skalski's scores on the port fuselage.

Another photo of the Skalski's Mustang III after combat mission, this time.

P-51B-7-NA (B-5 with fuselage tank installed after production). Aircraft s/n 43-7060, "Tommy's Dad" of 74th FS, 23rd FG, 14th AF, usually flown by John C. "Pappy" Herbst. Liuchow, China, 1944. Note hot air duct inlet cover seen only on the some P-51B-5. (US National Archives)

P-51B-5-NA, "Ticket Home" with hot air duct inlet cover and oil breathing exit in upper position. Note also dust filter covered with metal, ("blank door" used in the cold weather). (US National Archives)

P-51B-5-NA, s/n 43-6877, "The Stars Look Down" of the 355th FS, 354th FG at Criqueville airfield (A-2), France, 1944. The Mustang was modified by the 461st Air Service Squadron with a rumble seat. On 4 July 1944 MGen Quesada, Co 9th AF IX Fighter Command flew Gen. Eisenhower over the St. Lo combat sector. (US National Archives)

Malcolm hood canopy of the Mustang III, serial HB861, UZ-B, (P-51C-5-NT, s/n 42-103710). Personal aircraft of Flt. Lt. J Jeka, 306 Squadron PAF, March 1945. (Stratus coll.)

Most of the Mustang IIIs received British Mark II (and Mark IIL) gunsights.

Mustang III, serial FZ149, UZ-W, (P-51-B-5-NA, s/n 43-6530) of 306 Squadron PAF, photographed in October 1944. Note lack of the fuselage tank. (via W. Matusiak)

P-51B-1-NA in flight, view from above, showing shape of the Mustang wings. (NAA)

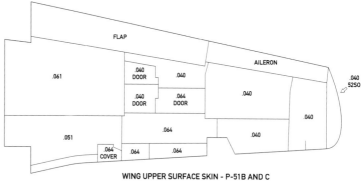

FLAP

AILERON

.061

.040
DOOR

.040

.040
52SO

.040
DOOR

.064
DOOR

.040

.040

.051

.064

.040

.064
COVER

.064

.064

WING UPPER SURFACE SKIN - P-51B AND C

NOTE:
ALL SKIN IS 24ST ALCAD EXCEPT AS
NOTED. DECIMAL FRACTIONS INDICATE
SKIN THICKNESS IN INCHES

FLAP

AILERON

.040
52SO

.040

.040

.061

.040

.040

.064

.040

.040

.064

.064

.040

.064

.064

.064

.064

*P-51B wing surface skins.
(Airplane Spare Catalog)*

WING LOWER SURFACE SKIN - P-51B AND C

COVER

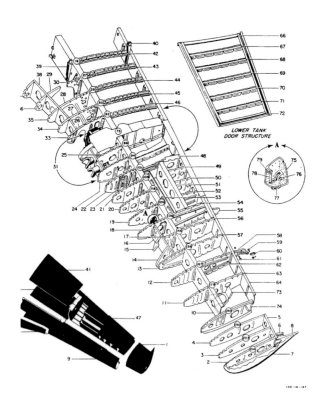

Wing structure.
(Airplane Spare Catalog)

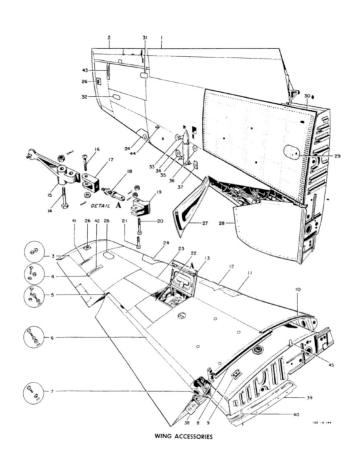

WING ACCESSORIES

Wing accesories, drawing from Parts Catalog.

P-51B station diagram, drawing from Spare Parts Catalog.

Aileron construction of P-51B/C, models 103, 104 & 111. Drawing from Spare Parts Catalog.

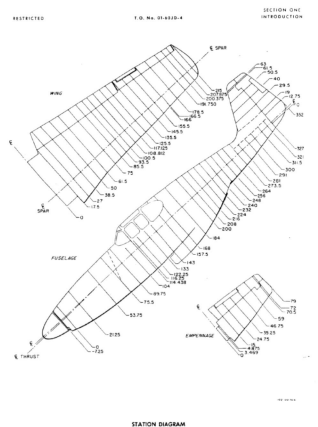

STATION DIAGRAM

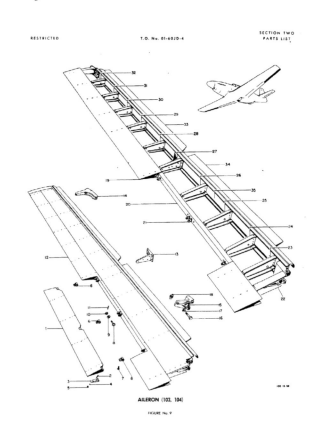

AILERON (103, 104)

FIGURE No. 9

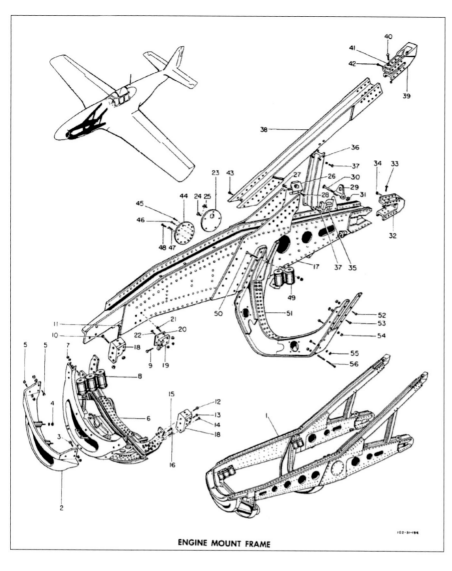

Engine mount frame.
(Airplane Parts Catalog)

ENGINE MOUNT FRAME

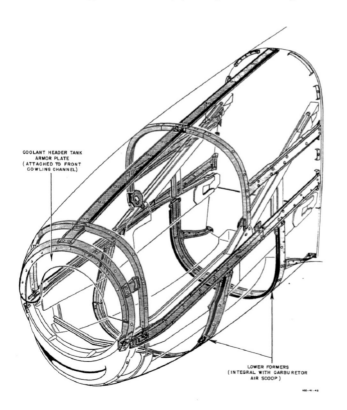

Engine cowling supports. (Both drawings from Airplane Parts Catalog)

COOLANT HEADER TANK
ARMOR PLATE
(ATTACHED TO FRONT
COWLING CHANNEL)

LOWER FORMERS
(INTEGRAL WITH CARBURETOR
AIR SCOOP)

Packard-built Rolls-Royce Merlin V-1650-3 engine details.
Photos from rection and Maintenance Instructions.

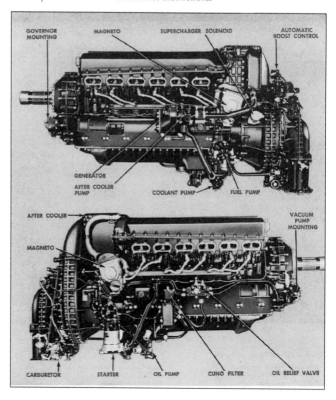

13

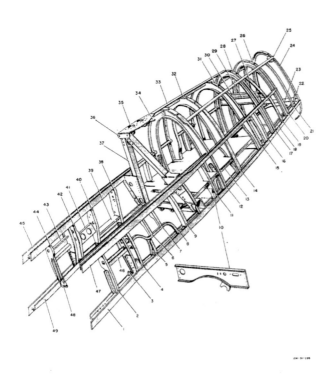

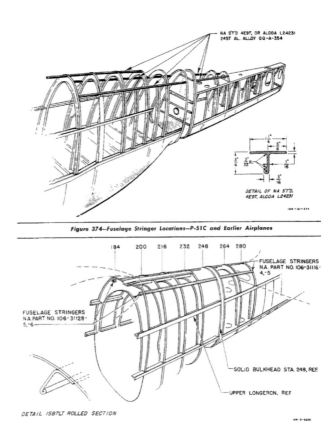

Figure 374—Fuselage Stringer Locations—P-51C and Earlier Airplanes

Above: Two drawings from Spare Parts Catalog showing fuselage construction.

Left: Radiator air scoop. Photo from Maintenance Manual P-51B&C.

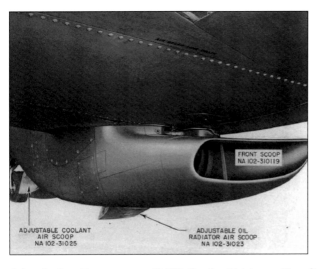

Drawing of the carburetor air scoop used on the models 104, 104 and 111. No. 18 is the hot air scoop used only on the some P-51B-5 series. (Airplane Parts Catalog)

Below: Fuselage skin arrangement of P-51B. (Based on Maintenance Manual)

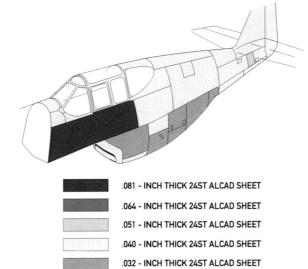

■	.081 - INCH THICK 24ST ALCAD SHEET
■	.064 - INCH THICK 24ST ALCAD SHEET
■	.051 - INCH THICK 24ST ALCAD SHEET
□	.040 - INCH THICK 24ST ALCAD SHEET
■	.032 - INCH THICK 24ST ALCAD SHEET

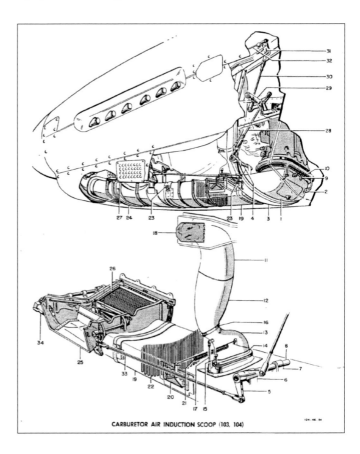

CARBURETOR AIR INDUCTION SCOOP (103, 104)

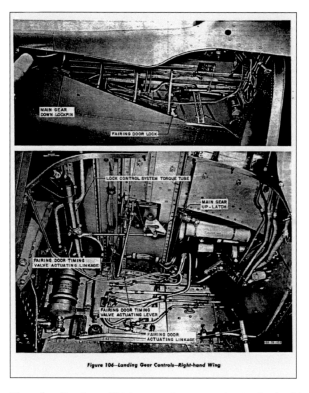
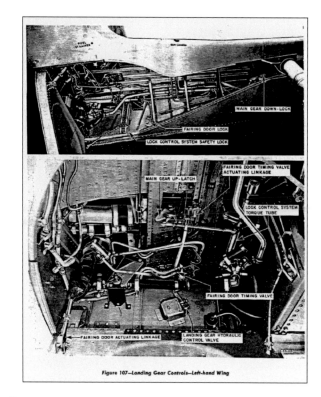

Photos from Erection and Maintenance Instructions showing details of the main wheel wells.

Below: Main gear fairing door.
(Erection and Maintenance Instructions)

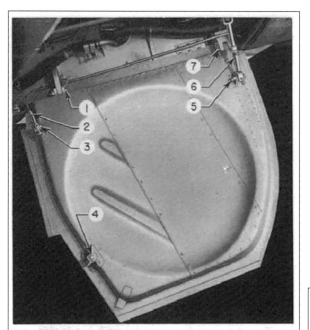

1. AN6-22 Bolt, AN310-6 Nut, and AN380-3-3 Cotter Key
2. 73-33340 Cable Assembly
3. AN5-10 Bolt, AN310-5 Nut, and AN380-2-2 Cotter Key
4. Fairing Door Locking Lug
5. AN6-16 Bolt, AN310-6 Nut, and AN380-3-3 Cotter Key
6. 73-33320 Link Assembly (LH)
   73-33320-1 Link Assembly (RH)
7. AN6-20 Bolt, AN310-6 Nut, and AN380-3-3 Cotter Key

Figure 111—Main Gear Fairing Door

Main undercarriage leg.
(Erection and Mainte-
nance Instructions)

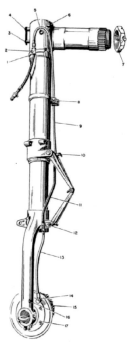

Tail gear details, latch mechanism and fairing
doors are shown.
(Erection and Maintenance Instructions)

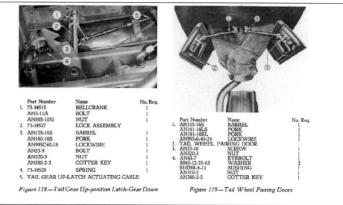

Part Number	Name	No. Req.
1. 73-34515	BELLCRANK	1
AN3-11A	BOLT	1
AN365-1032	NUT	1
2. 73-34527	LOCK ASSEMBLY	1
3. AN155-16S	BARREL	1
AN160-16S	FORK	1
AN995C40-18	LOCKWIRE	1
AN23-9	BOLT	1
AN320-3	NUT	1
AN380-2-2	COTTER KEY	1
4. 73-34528	SPRING	1
5. TAIL GEAR UP-LATCH ACTUATING CABLE		

Figure 118—Tail Gear Up-position Latch-Gear Down

Part Number	Name	No. Req.
1. AN155-16S	BARREL	1
AN161-16LS	FORK	1
AN161-16RL	FORK	1
AN995-6-40-24	LOCKWIRE	1
2. TAIL WHEEL FAIRING DOOR		
3. AN23-10	SCREW	1
AN320-3	NUT	1
4. AN43-7	EYEBOLT	2
B985-12-20-63	WASHER	1
B1009R-4-11	BUSHING	1
AN310-3	NUT	1
AN380-2-2	COTTER KEY	1

Figure 119—Tail Wheel Fairing Doors

Starboard wing guns installation. (Maintenance Manual)

1. FEED CHUTES
2. GUN HEATERS
3. EJECTION CHUTES
4. REAR MOUNTING POST
5. TYPE G-11 SOLENOID
6. ASBESTOS LAGGING (GUN HEATER WIRE)

Below, left: *Port wing ammunition compartment.*

Below, right: *Port wing guns installed. (Maintenance Manual)*

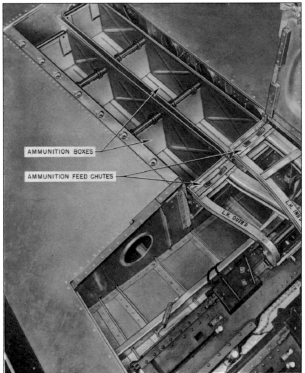

AMMUNITION BOXES

AMMUNITION FEED CHUTES

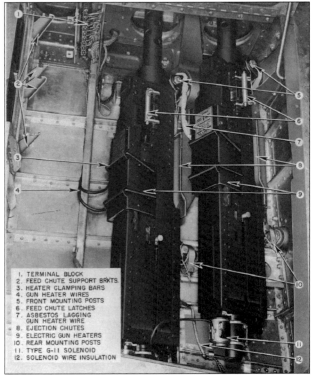

1. TERMINAL BLOCK
2. FEED CHUTE SUPPORT BRKTS.
3. HEATER CLAMPING BARS
4. GUN HEATER WIRES
5. FRONT MOUNTING POSTS
6. FEED CHUTE LATCHES
7. ASBESTOS LAGGING GUN HEATER WIRE
8. EJECTION CHUTES
9. ELECTRIC GUN HEATERS
10. REAR MOUNTING POSTS
11. TYPE G-11 SOLENOID
12. SOLENOID WIRE INSULATION

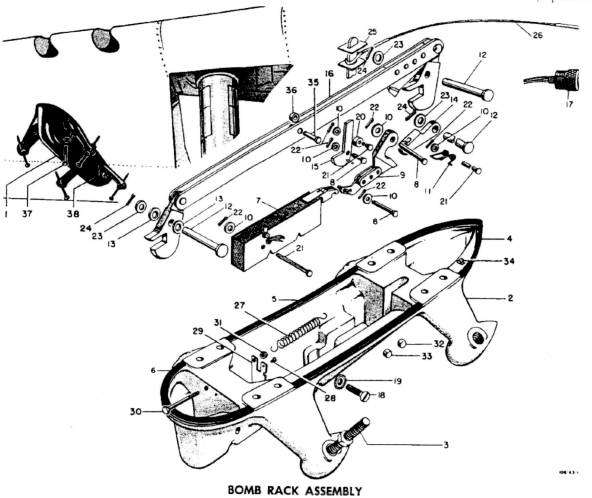

BOMB RACK ASSEMBLY

Bomb installed on the bomb rack. (Maintenance Manual)

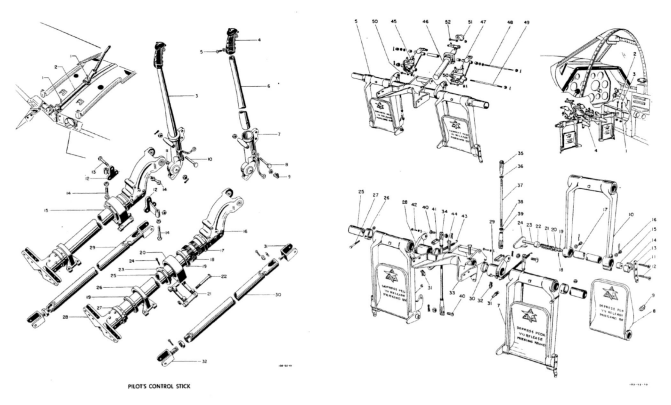

PILOT'S CONTROL STICK

Above: Control stick assembly. (Airplane Parts Catalog) Above, right: Rudder pedals assembly. (Airplane Parts Catalog)
Below: Preserved P-51B-10-NA, s/n 42-106638, "Impatient Virgin". Details of the instrument panel. The same layout was in B-5 version. (R. Malmstrom)

18

Malcom hood canopy an the preserved P-51B. Note the ground jack under fuselage fuel filler cap. (R. Boullier)

P-51B-5-NA Mustang III instrument panel.

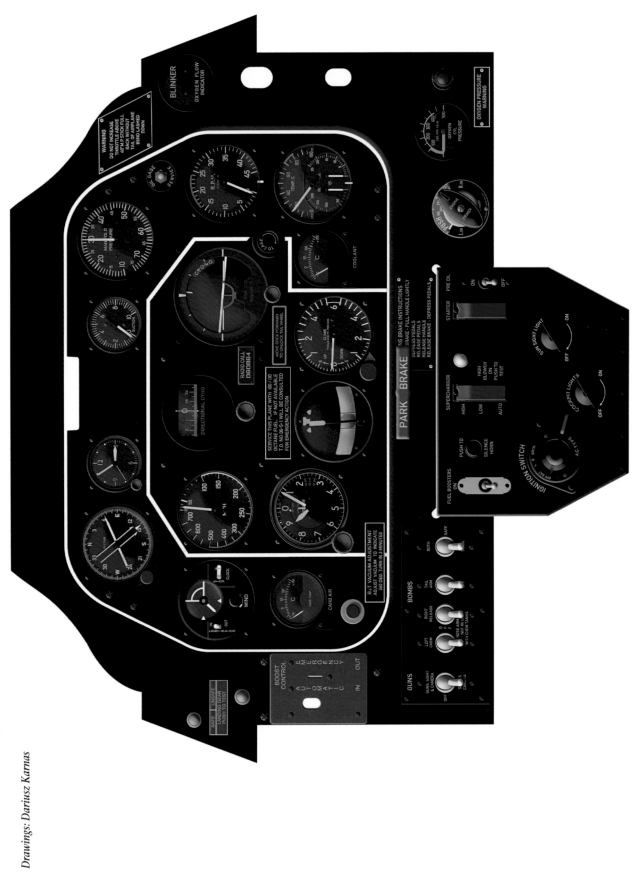

Drawings: Dariusz Karnas

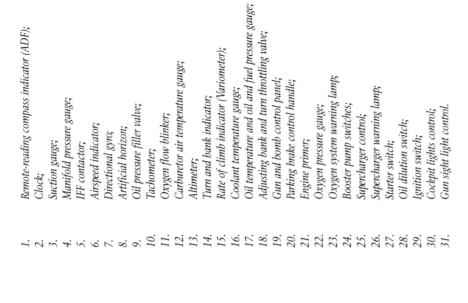

1. Remote-reading compass indicator (ADF);
2. Clock;
3. Suction gauge;
4. Manifold pressure gauge;
5. IFF contactor;
6. Airspeed indicator;
7. Directional gyro;
8. Artificial horizon;
9. Oil pressure filler valve;
10. Tachometer;
11. Oxygen flow blinker;
12. Carburetor air temperature gauge;
13. Altimeter;
14. Turn and bank indicator;
15. Rate of climb indicator (Variometer);
16. Coolant temperature gauge;
17. Oil temperature and oil and fuel pressure gauge;
18. Adjusting bank and turn throttling valve;
19. Gun and bomb control panel;
20. Parking brake control handle;
21. Engine primer;
22. Oxygen pressure gauge;
23. Oxygen system warning lamp;
24. Booster pump switches;
25. Supercharger control;
26. Supercharger warning lamp;
27. Starter switch;
28. Oil dilution switch;
29. Ignition switch;
30. Cockpit lights control;
31. Gun sight light control.

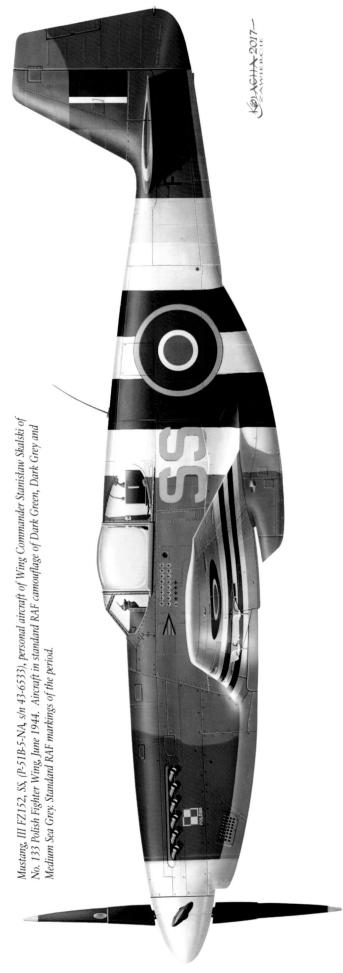

Mustang, III FZ152, SS, (P-51B-5-NA s/n 43-6533), personal aircraft of Wing Commander Stanisław Skalski of No. 133 Polish Fighter Wing, June 1944. Aircraft in standard RAF camouflage of Dark Green, Dark Grey and Medium Sea Grey. Standard RAF markings of the period.

22

Zbigniew Kolacha

Mustang, III FZ152, SS, (P-51B-5-NA, s/n 43-6533), personal aircraft of Wing
Commander Stanisław Skalski of No. 133 Polish Fighter Wing, June 1944.

Zbigniew Kolacha

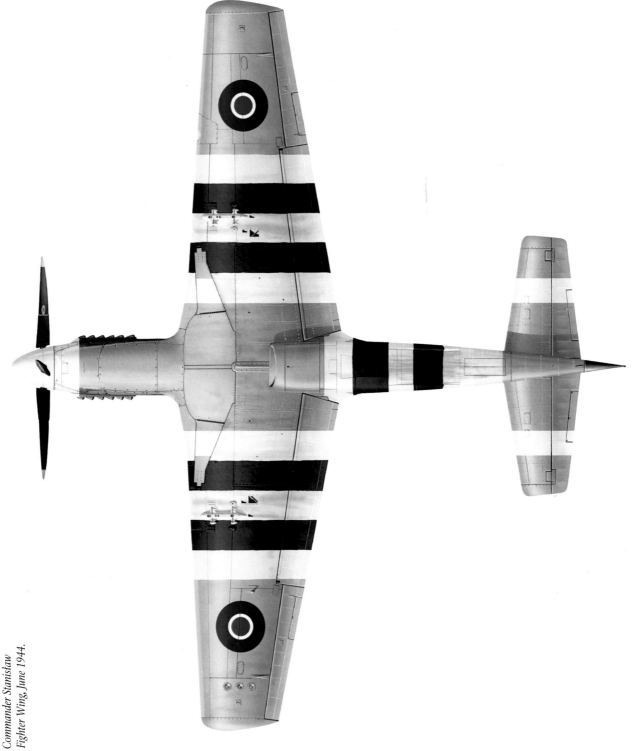

*Mustang, III FZ152, SS, (P-51B-5-NA, s/n 43-6533),
personal aircraft of Wing Commander Stanisław
Skalski of No. 133 Polish Fighter Wing, June 1944.*

Zbigniew Kolacha

24